POWERFUL MISSILES AND BOMBS

ARNOLD RINGSTAD

Published by The Child's World®
800-599-READ • www.childsworld.com

Copyright © 2024 by The Child's World®
All rights reserved. No part of this book may be reproduced or utilized in any form or by any means without written permission from the publisher.

Photography Credits
Photographs ©: Cpl. Sean Evans/Alaskan NORAD Region/Alaskan Command/11th Air Force/US Marine Corps/DVIDS, cover, 1; US Air Force, 3; Tech. Sgt. Matthew Plew/48th Fighter Wing Public Affairs/US Air Force/DVIDS, 5; Sgt. T. T. Parish/II Marine Expeditionary Force/DVIDS, 6; Staff Sgt. Lee F. Corkran/US Air Force, 9; Lance Cpl. Alyssa Chuluda/US Army Pacific Public Affairs Office/US Marine Corps/DVIDS, 11; Visual Information Specialist Markus Rauchenberger/Training Support Activity Europe/US Army/DVIDS, 13; Airman Nathan Barbour/355th Wing/US Air Force/DVIDS, 14; CTBTO/Science Source, 17; Red Line Editorial, 18; Seaman Benjamin Crossley/US Navy, 20

ISBN Information
9781503816732 (Reinforced Library Binding)
9781503881426 (Portable Document Format)
9781503882737 (Online Multi-user eBook)
9781503884045 (Electronic Publication)

LCCN 2022922689

Printed in the United States of America

ABOUT THE AUTHOR

Arnold Ringstad is a writer and editor who lives in Minnesota. He enjoys reading about military history and technology.

CONTENTS

CHAPTER ONE
FOX THREE! 4

CHAPTER TWO
MISSILES 8

CHAPTER THREE
BOMBS 12

CHAPTER FOUR
NUCLEAR WEAPONS 16

Glossary . . . 22
Fast Facts . . . 23
One Stride Further . . . 23
Find Out More . . . 24
Index . . . 24

CHAPTER ONE

FOX THREE!

It is June 30, 2022. High over the Gulf of Mexico, an F-15E Strike Eagle zooms through the sky. The fighter jet's twin engines roar. Its two-person crew looks out over the blue horizon. They are searching for their target.

The pilot spots the target near the Florida coast. It is a small jet called a QF-16. It is a target drone. This means it is controlled remotely. There are no people inside. The Strike Eagle's crew members press buttons in their **cockpit**. Their plane's **radar** locks onto the QF-16.

Full-weapon system demonstrations are tests that use real ammunition. They show the military that missiles will work in combat.

Crew members make sure that missiles have been loaded correctly during preflight safety checks.

A missile is hanging under the Strike Eagle's wing. This missile is a new version of the AIM-120 Advanced Medium-Range Air-to-Air Missile (AMRAAM). The AIM-120 is an air-to-air missile. This means that aircraft use it to shoot down other aircraft. The new model the crew is using is called the AIM-120D3. It is about 7 feet (2.1 m) long. It weighs about 330 pounds (150 kg).

★ ★ ★

The pilot calls out "Fox Three!" on his radio. This code means he is firing a radar-guided missile. The AIM-120D3 falls away from the Strike Eagle. Then its rocket motor blasts the missile to **supersonic** speed. The missile has its own radar system. It steers itself toward the target. The missile reaches the QF-16 and explodes. The flaming target drone falls into the sea. Today's test is a success.

The US Air Force has used versions of the AIM-120 since 1991. The missile has received many upgrades over time. The AIM-120D3 includes more advanced computer chips and software than previous models. This technology helps the missile track its targets. Developing this new missile cost about $125 million. The June 2022 test was the first of five test launches. The military relies on successful tests to decide whether new missiles can be used on real missions.

The AIM-120D3 is one of many missiles and bombs in the US military's **arsenal**. These weapons are used against enemy planes, tanks, buildings, and other targets. Advanced technology helps the missiles find and hit these targets. Missiles and bombs are some of the most powerful weapons used today.

CHAPTER TWO

MISSILES

The US military uses many kinds of missiles. Some are fired by a single soldier at close range. Others need a huge launcher and can travel many miles. Some missiles are also shot from airplanes or submarines. The military chooses different missiles for different missions and targets.

Fighter jets use the AIM-9 Sidewinder missile to shoot down other aircraft. The military first used this missile in the 1950s. It has seen many improvements since then. The latest version is the AIM-9X. The Sidewinder is a heat-seeking missile. It steers itself toward the hot engines of enemy aircraft. Pilots can fire it, then fly away to safety while the missile finds the target. Each Sidewinder is about 9.5 feet (2.9 m) long. The missile weighs 190 pounds (86 kg).

Aircraft can carry multiple kinds of missiles and bombs at the same time. Some jets carry two AIM-9 Sidewinders on each side.

Aircraft also attack ground targets. They can use the AGM-65 Maverick missile for these missions. Some Mavericks are heat-seeking. Others are laser-guided. This means the plane shines a laser beam at the target. The missile sees the laser and follows it. Some Mavericks are more powerful than others. Each Maverick weighs up to 800 pounds (363 kg). That includes up to 300 pounds (136 kg) of explosives.

Other missiles are fired from the ground. The MIM-104 Patriot is one of these. It was originally made to attack aircraft. Later upgrades let it shoot down enemy missiles, too. Patriot missiles use radar to find and track targets. The missiles are 17 feet (5.2 m) long. The heaviest versions weigh almost 2,000 pounds (900 kg).

THE JAVELIN

The FGM-148 Javelin missile is fired by a single soldier using a heavy shoulder launcher. The Javelin is designed to attack enemy tanks. The missile flies high into the air, then strikes the target from above. This is where a tank's armor is the weakest. The Javelin has a range of more than 1.5 miles (2.4 km).

Each Patriot launching station can hold and fire multiple missiles.

The MGM-140 Army Tactical Missile System (ATACMS) is a surface-to-surface missile. This means it is fired from the ground and attacks targets on the ground. Soldiers launch the missile from a truck. The missile then uses the **Global Positioning System (GPS)** to find the targets. While the missile is in the air, it makes sudden movements back and forth. This makes it harder for enemies to track. An ATACMS missile weighs 3,680 pounds (1,670 kg). It can hit targets 186 miles (300 km) away.

CHAPTER THREE

BOMBS

The US military mainly uses three basic types of bombs. The Mark 82 weighs 500 pounds (227 kg). The Mark 83 weighs 1,000 pounds (454 kg). And the Mark 84 weighs 2,000 pounds (907 kg). These bombs are unguided. That means they cannot steer themselves to a target. The pilot simply drops them on the enemy. These are sometimes called "dumb bombs."

However, the military can turn any of these weapons into "smart bombs." Smart bombs can steer themselves to targets with the addition of computers and fins. This equipment makes the bombs much more accurate.

CARRYING BOMBS
The B-2 Spirit is one of the US military's bomber aircraft. These planes are specially designed to drop bombs. Each B-2 can carry up to 80 Mark 82 bombs. That adds up to 40,000 pounds (18,100 kg) of bombs carried by a single aircraft.

A standard Mark 82 bomb is deadly up to 130 feet (40 m) away from where it lands.

Fins can be added to bombs at military bases. Soldiers attach the type of fin that is the best fit for the mission.

A few different kinds of equipment can be added to bombs. One is the Joint Direct Attack Munition (JDAM). It lets the bomb use GPS to find a target. The pilot types in the **coordinates** of the target. The aircraft sends this information to the computer on the bomb. As the bomb falls, the fins steer it to that location. However, the bomb's improved accuracy comes at a cost. Each JDAM kit costs about $30,000.

Paveway III is another attachment kit that makes bombs more accurate. It lets the pilot use a laser to guide the bomb to its target. Paveway III bombs can hit targets from a height of 33,000 feet (10,000 m). Adding the Paveway III kit to a bomb can cost up to $70,000.

The US military also uses some much larger bombs. These are designed to attack challenging targets, such as **bunkers**. One of the biggest is the GBU-43B Massive Ordnance Air Blast (MOAB). It is also nicknamed "Mother of All Bombs." This huge bomb weighs 22,600 pounds (10,250 kg). The MOAB is the largest nonnuclear bomb ever used in combat.

CHAPTER FOUR

NUCLEAR WEAPONS

Nuclear weapons are the most powerful weapons on Earth. They work by splitting **atoms**. This releases a huge amount of energy. Part of this energy causes a huge explosion. The process also gives off harmful energy called **radiation**.

Nuclear weapons are powerful enough to destroy entire cities. Only two of them have ever been used in war. The United States dropped two separate nuclear bombs on Japan near the end of World War II (1939–1945). Together, the bombs killed more than 130,000 people.

Today, many nations have nuclear weapons. The United States has three basic types. One type is bombs dropped from airplanes. Another is missiles launched from land. And the third is missiles launched from submarines.

The United States has completed more than 1,000 nuclear weapon tests.

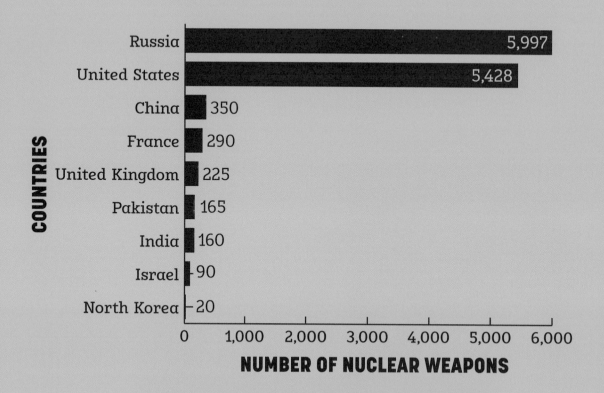

This graph shows the estimated number of nuclear weapons owned by different countries in 2022, according to the Federation of American Scientists.

Nuclear **warheads** are far more powerful than regular bombs. The explosive power of nuclear weapons is measured in kilotons. One kiloton is equal to the power of 1,000 tons of the common explosive TNT. Even a small nuclear weapon can create a gigantic explosion.

The US military's nuclear bombs are the B61 and the B83. Bombers such as the B-52 or the B-2 can drop these bombs. A parachute slows the bombs' fall. This gives the aircraft time to fly away before the bomb explodes. The B61 has an explosive power of 400 kilotons. The B83 is even bigger, at 1,200 kilotons. By comparison, the bombs dropped on Japan had about 20 kilotons of power.

The United States also uses Minuteman III missiles. These launch from underground bases. Each missile weighs about 80,000 pounds (36,300 kg). They can travel more than 6,000 miles (9,700 km). This means they can hit a target almost anywhere on Earth. A Minuteman III missile carries a single warhead.

★ ★ ★

20

The US Navy's Trident II missiles launch from submarines. Submarines can get close to enemy shores before firing. The Trident II is 44 feet (13.4 m) long. A single submarine can carry up to 20 of them. Each missile can carry more than one warhead. Those warheads can hit different targets. This makes the Trident II an especially powerful weapon.

The US military has many kinds of explosives in its arsenal. Small missiles, huge bombs, and nuclear warheads all have different purposes. New weapons are always being created, too. In the future, there might be weapons that are even more powerful than those of today.

The US Navy test launches unarmed Trident II missiles. The military can make sure the system works without causing explosions.

GLOSSARY

arsenal (AR-suh-null) An arsenal is the complete group of weapons that a military has. The US military has a large arsenal with a variety of weapons.

atoms (AT-umz) Atoms are the smallest particles that make up matter. Atoms are the building blocks for everything in the universe.

bunkers (BUNK-urz) Bunkers are structures that protect people. The military bunkers were made of concrete and protected soldiers from the blast.

cockpit (KOK-pit) The cockpit is the part of the aircraft where the pilot sits. Pilots use controls in the cockpit to fire missiles and drop bombs.

coordinates (koh-OR-duh-nuts) Coordinates are a set of numbers that are used to show a location on a map. The missile used coordinates to find and hit the target.

Global Positioning System (GPS) (GLOH-bul puh-ZIH-shuh-ning SISS-tuhm) GPS uses satellites to help devices on Earth figure out where the device is located. Some bombs use GPS to help them locate and hit targets.

radar (RAY-dar) Radar is equipment that sends out signals and then detects the reflections of those signals after they bounce off objects. Some missiles use radar to help track the location and speed of their targets.

radiation (ray-dee-AY-shun) Radiation is energy that moves from one place to another. The nuclear bomb gave off dangerous radiation.

supersonic (soo-per-SAH-nik) Supersonic means something is faster than the speed of sound, about 760 miles per hour (1,225 kmh) at sea level. Many missiles travel at supersonic speed.

warheads (WAR-hedz) Warheads are explosive devices. There are nuclear warheads at the tip of a Trident II missile.

FAST FACTS

★ The US military uses missiles and bombs to attack enemy targets in the air and on the ground.

★ Some missiles are small and can be fired by a single soldier. Others require large launchers and can reach targets from many miles away.

★ Laser guidance, radar, and GPS are some of the ways missiles and bombs find targets.

★ Nuclear weapons are the most powerful weapons on Earth. The US military's nuclear weapons include bombs, missiles launched from the ground, and missiles launched from submarines.

ONE STRIDE FURTHER

★ There are many kinds of missiles. How do you think the military decides which missiles to use for certain missions?

★ Building smart bombs is expensive. Do you think advanced tracking devices are worth their cost?

★ Nuclear weapons are controversial. Some people think that having nuclear weapons stops large wars from starting, since the destruction from using these weapons would be too terrible. Other people think that countries with nuclear weapons should give them up because they are too dangerous. Do you think these unique weapons are necessary? Why or why not?

FIND OUT MORE

IN THE LIBRARY

Billings, Tanner. *The U.S. Air Force*. New York, NY: Rosen, 2022.

Brallier, Jess M. *What Was the Bombing of Hiroshima?* New York, NY: Penguin Workshop, 2020.

Henzel, Cynthia Kennedy. *Powerful Military Aircraft*. Parker, CO: The Child's World, 2024.

ON THE WEB

Visit our website for links about missiles and bombs:

childsworld.com/links

Note to Parents, Caregivers, Teachers, and Librarians: We routinely verify our Web links to make sure they are safe and active sites. So encourage your readers to check them out!

INDEX

AGM-65 Maverick, 10
AIM-9 Sidewinder, 8
AIM-120 AMRAAM, 6–7

GBU-43B MOAB, 15

Mark 82, 12
Mark 83, 12
Mark 84, 12
MIM-104 Patriot, 10
Minuteman III, 19

nuclear weapons, 16, 18–19, 21

Paveway III, 15

radar, 4, 7, 10

submarines, 8, 16, 21

targets, 4, 7, 8, 10–11, 12, 15, 19, 21
Trident II, 21